Forces and Motion

by Jane Weir

Science Contributor
Sally Ride Science

Science Consultant
Michael E. Kopecky, Science Educator

MISSION: SCIENCE

Sally Ride
Science

Sally Ride Science™ is an innovative content company dedicated to fueling young people's interests in science.

Our publications and programs provide opportunities for students and teachers to explore the captivating world of science—from astrobiology to zoology.

We bring science to life and show young people that science is creative, collaborative, fascinating, and fun.

To learn more, visit www.SallyRideScience.com

First hardcover edition published in 2009 by
Compass Point Books
151 Good Counsel Drive
P.O. Box 669
Mankato, MN 56002-0669

Editor: Robert McConnell
Designer: Heidi Thompson
Editorial Contributor: Sue Vander Hook

Art Director: LuAnn Ascheman-Adams
Creative Director: Joe Ewest
Editorial Director: Nick Healy
Managing Editor: Catherine Neitge

 This book was manufactured with paper containing at least 10 percent post-consumer waste.

Library of Congress Cataloging-in-Publication Data
Weir, Jane, 1976–
  Forces and motion / by Jane Weir.—1st hardcover ed.
     p. cm.—(Mission: Science)
  Includes index.
  ISBN 978-0-7565-4228-3 (library binding)
  1. Force and energy—Juvenile literature. 2. Motion—Juvenile literature.
  I. Title. II. Series.
  QC73.4.W434 2009
  531'.11—dc22   2009003673

Visit Compass Point Books on the Internet at *www.compasspointbooks.com*
or e-mail your request to *custserv@compasspointbooks.com*

Table of Contents

Forces Make Things Happen

Without motion, the world would be a very boring place. Earth wouldn't spin, people wouldn't run, and leaves wouldn't fall. In fact, nothing would move at all. But our world is full of motion. Forces are responsible for making things move.

Until a force acts on a motionless object, the object just sits there. A leaf on the ground is at rest unless a force, such as the wind, makes it move. Forces cannot be seen, but their effects are often obvious. Objects speed up, slow down, or change direction or shape when forces are at work.

We use forces all the time. The force of our muscles on our bones makes us move. When you kick a ball, your foot's force makes the ball

Measuring Force

Force can be measured by using a Newton meter, which is also called a spring scale. Inside the meter is a spring that stretches when a force pulls on it. The stronger the force, the more the spring stretches. You can hang something from the scale to find out what it weighs.

Did You Know?

The unit used to measure force is called a newton. It's named for Isaac Newton, an English scientist and mathematician. He discovered some of the most important things in science—the law of gravity and the three laws of motion. These laws explain how forces work.

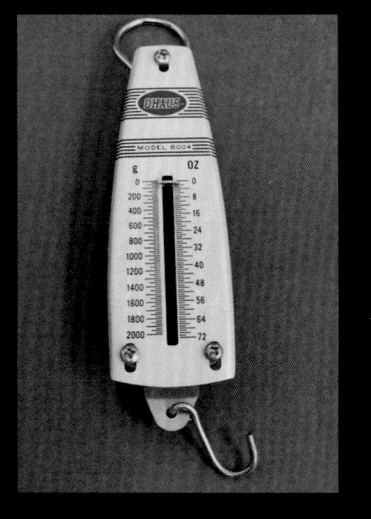

fly into the air. Your weight is a measurement of force. Your body is pulled toward Earth by gravity. Without this important force, you would float into space.

There are four basic forces: gravity, electromagnetic force, and what scientists call the strong force and the weak force. Gravity is the best known of these, but all of them are very important.

Electromagnetic force holds atoms together in molecules. It also keeps protons and electrons in their places. The strong force keeps protons and neutrons in the center of atoms, while the weak force changes one kind of atomic particle into another. Without forces, the universe would be a sea of particles.

Forces move bodies and soccer balls.

Moon Diet?

Mass is the amount of matter (what many people would call "stuff") of which something is made. Your mass is the same wherever you are in the universe. Mass is not the same as weight. Your weight measures the force that gravity exerts on your mass. So weight changes when gravity changes.

On the moon, gravity is only one-sixth as strong as it is on Earth. Your moon weight would be only one-sixth of that on Earth, but your mass would be the same. A person who weighs 100 pounds (45 kilograms) on Earth would weigh about 16 pounds (7 kg) on the moon. That would make it easy for you to jump high on the moon.

Balanced Forces

More than one force can act on an object at the same time. When that happens, there is something like a tug-of-war between the forces. One force might be pushing while another force is pulling. The stronger of the two forces will move the object in the direction in which the force is applied.

Sometimes the forces are the same. A swing hanging motionless is being affected by two equal but opposite forces. Gravity is pulling the swing down, and the chains or ropes are pulling it up. The swing doesn't move even though two forces are working on it.

If all the forces acting on an object are balanced, then the object will either remain still or keep doing what it was doing. When forces are balanced, the object is said to be in equilibrium. A chandelier hanging from the ceiling is in equilibrium—

the downward force of gravity is balanced by an upward force from the chain holding the chandelier. The chandelier stays still.

Other examples of equilibrium are a football lying on the ground and an apple on a tree. In fact, any object at rest is in equilibrium. So is a floating boat. The upward push of the water balances the weight of the boat and keeps it from sinking.

One Big Theory

Scientists are trying to find a way to describe the universe by linking all the forces into one. They call such a description the grand unified theory. They haven't found a way to combine all the forces into one theory yet, but they're still working on the problem.

If the forces on an object are not equal or balanced, then the object will change speed or direction, or both. When you kick a ball, your foot provides a force greater than the force of gravity on the ball. The ball moves quickly through the air. When you push a child on a swing, your arms supply the force to make the swing move.

The ball and the swing both move in the direction in which the force pushes them. When a force acts on an object that is already moving, the object will speed up, slow down, change direction, or change both speed and direction. The stronger the force, the bigger the effect on the object.

If you push something hard, it will speed up more than if you just give it a little tap. If you pedal hard on your bike, you will speed up more than if you push the pedals gently.

The same thing happens in reverse when braking. A little pressure from the brakes won't slow your bike much. To make it stop, you might have to squeeze the brake levers as hard as you can.

◄ Pushing a small child on a swing is easy for most people because not much force is needed.

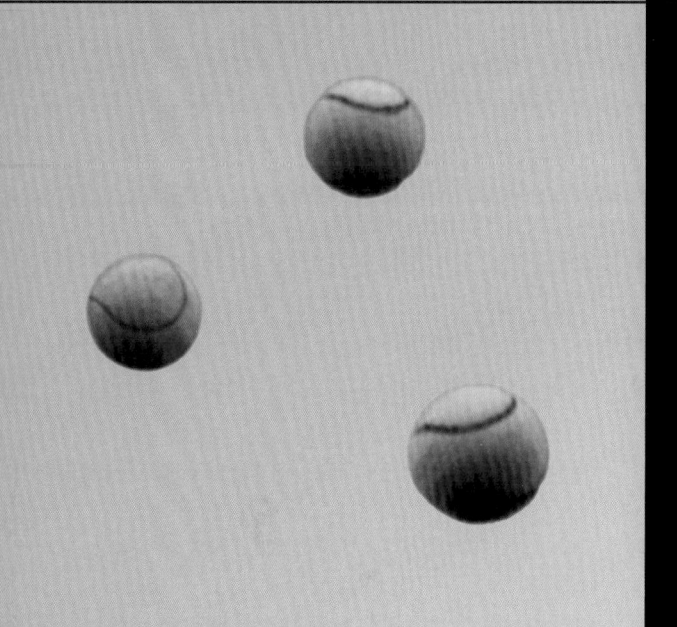

When Does a Juggling Ball Move the Fastest?

The speed of a juggling ball is greatest when it leaves the juggler's hand and when it returns to a hand. The hand delivers the upward force, and gravity hurries it back downward. The ball's lowest speed is at the top of its path, when it stops for a split second and changes direction because of gravity.

Speed and Acceleration

Speed is how far something moves in a certain amount of time. It is measured in distance (such as miles or kilometers) per unit of time (such as hours). For example, a car on a highway might travel 65 miles (105 km) per hour. It moves because the engine exerts a force on the car's wheels and tires, and they exert a force on the road. More force is needed to move a big car than to move a small car.

When the amount of force changes, so does the speed of the car. If there is more force, the car accelerates—speeds up. You can see why the gas pedal is called the accelerator. Acceleration is measured by how quickly an object changes speed. A driver pushes down hard on the gas pedal to create a lot of acceleration. Pushing down gently creates just a little acceleration.

To make the car decelerate—slow down—a little, the driver can reduce the force by not pushing as hard on the gas pedal. Not pushing on the pedal at all makes the car slow down even more,

Fighter pilots can accelerate their planes very quickly. The strong force created by the acceleration makes blood rush from their heads to their legs, which can make them dizzy. It's not safe to fly a plane when you're dizzy. To prevent this, fighter pilots wear special pants. The pants inflate and press on their legs. The pressure keeps the extra blood from running into their legs.

and eventually it will stop moving. Brakes can stop the car faster, because they apply a strong force in the opposite direction.

Rubbery Face

When stunt pilots, such as the Navy's Blue Angels, fly their planes in a loop, the skin on the pilots' faces becomes distorted. The force of flying in an up-and-down circle causes the skin to accelerate and get pushed out of shape. Skin is stretchy, and facial skin is not strongly attached to anything. So it accelerates more than what's under it. When a plane comes out of a loop, the extra force stops and the pilot's face returns to normal.

Friction and Resistance

Friction is a force that slows things down or keeps them from moving. It happens where surfaces touch each other. The force of friction always pushes opposite the direction of an object's motion. When you slide your hand across the top of a table, you can feel friction keeping your hand from sliding easily. Water is slippery, but friction happens when a boat moves through it.

Air resistance is a type of friction that presses against anything moving through air. Airplane engines need to create enough force to push forward harder than air resistance is pushing backward. Air resistance is also called drag. It is what lets a parachute slow a skydiver's fall.

Friction is often a very good thing. We need friction to walk, because it provides a

grip between the ground and our feet. Walking on slippery ice is dangerous because there's a lot less friction. Without friction, objects that we tried to pick up would just slip out of our hands. Tires need friction to hold vehicles on the road.

But friction also can cause problems. Friction between moving parts of machines, such as gears, causes grinding and heat. The machines don't work as well, and eventually the friction wears out the parts. The friction can be greatly reduced, though, by using lubrication, such as applying oil to the parts. Without oil, a lot of machines would stop working.

Friction Addiction

Rock climbers depend on the force of friction to keep themselves from falling. Friction between a climber's hands and feet and the rock helps the climber stay on the rock and continue to climb. The upward force from muscles in the climber's arms, hands, legs, and feet balances the downward force of gravity. Rock climbers wear sticky, flexible rubber shoes to create a lot of friction between their shoes and the rock.

Did You Know?

Objects moving through water experience more friction than objects moving through the air. That's because water is denser than air. The tiny particles that make up water are more tightly packed than the particles in air. More force is needed to move through water than through air, and it's even harder to move an object with a rough surface through water. To reduce friction between their bodies and the water, fish and other sea creatures often have smooth, slippery surfaces.

Newton's Laws of Motion

Isaac Newton, an English scientist and mathematician, published a book in 1687 that contains some of the most important scientific writings of all time. The book explains gravity and describes three laws of motion. Laws, in science, state something that scientists believe is always true.

Newton's first law of motion is also called the law of inertia. Inertia means resistance to motion. In modern English, the law says:

> *An object that is at rest or moving steadily in a straight line will stay that way until an outside force acts on it.*

This means that an object that isn't moving will not move until a force makes it move. A leaf that falls from a tree will stay where it lands unless something moves it, such as the wind. The leaf, like all objects at rest, has inertia.

An object moving in a straight line also has inertia, Newton said. It will keep moving that way until a force makes it move differently or stop. If you hit a baseball, it starts moving in a straight line. The ball will go on in that straight line until gravity, air resistance, or a baseball glove stops the ball or slows it down.

Newton's second law of motion describes what happens when a force acts on an object:

> *A change in an object's motion depends on the amount of force applied to it, the direction in which the force moves, and the mass of the object.*

The second law means three things. One is that it takes more force to create

Trachette Jackson, Ph.D.

To do his work, Isaac Newton created a new kind of mathematics called calculus. Calculus is important for almost every scientist. Trachette Jackson, a professor at the University of Michigan, uses it in her field, mathematical biology. Calculus helps her to study cancer cells. The more she knows, the closer she comes to learning how cancer can be stopped. Newton's important work helps today's scientists do important work.

more acceleration. Second, force makes an object move in the same direction in which the force is moving. Third, it's harder to accelerate a heavy object (one with more mass) than a light object.

Here's an example of how the law works: The harder you hit a baseball, the faster it goes. The direction the bat is moving in is the direction in which the ball goes. A baseball moves faster when hit than a bowling ball hit the same way.

Blown Away

Newton's second law explains why leaves are blown around more than sticks. Leaves have less mass than sticks. They also catch a lot more wind. With less mass and more force, leaves accelerate much more easily than sticks do.

Newton's third law of motion describes actions and reactions. It says:

For every action, there is an equal and opposite reaction.

This means that when a force is exerted on an object, the object exerts force in return. You can experience this by pushing on a wall. Your hands don't go through the wall because the wall is applying an equal force back. The pressure you feel on your hands is the force or reaction of the wall. You can also feel reaction force when you sit on a chair. Your weight pushes down on the chair because of gravity, but the chair's reaction force pushes up, balancing your weight.

Reaction force is how rockets are propelled through space. A rocket's engine pushes a mass of exhaust gases out the back. The force that the rocket applies to the exhaust is the same as the force of the exhaust on the rocket. The two push each other apart, which makes the rocket go forward.

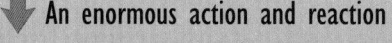
An enormous action and reaction

USA
NASA
Discovery

The First Rocketeers

The Chinese were the first people to experiment with rockets because they were the first to have gunpowder. Rockets need a force such as gunpowder to propel them into space. As early as 1150, the Chinese were using gunpowder to power rockets.

Why Do Airplanes Need a Runway?

As an airplane moves forward, air flows over and under its wings. A wing is made so the air going over the top travels farther than the air going under the wing. The faster-moving air on top of the wing is less dense (it has less pressure) than the air below. This pressure difference is what allows flight.

The force upward, called lift, is bigger than the force downward, so the wing rises. When the plane moves faster, its lift increases. To create lift and fly into the sky, airplanes need to move quickly down the runway. Heavy planes need a lot more lift than light planes. So big planes need longer runways to gain enough speed to lift off the ground.

Air spread out = less pressure.

Air close together = more pressure.

The Force of Gravity

Gravity is a force. But it's different from most other forces because it can only pull things together. It can't push them apart.

Some people might think gravity is just the force that keeps things on Earth from floating into space. Gravity does do that, but it also does a lot more.

Isaac Newton described gravity as the attraction any two objects in the universe have for each other. Gravity can't always be felt, but it's always there.

It's a good thing, too. The enormous force of the sun's gravity is what keeps Earth and all the other planets in their orbits. Earth's gravity keeps the moon in orbit around our planet. Newton was the first person to realize that the force that makes the moon orbit Earth is the same force that makes things on Earth fall to the ground.

Without gravity, the moon would float away from Earth.

gravitational pull

Falling to the Center

On Earth things that are falling look as though they are going downward. Actually they are falling toward the center of Earth. At the very center of the planet, the force of gravity is the same in all directions. If you could go there, you might think gravity had disappeared, because you wouldn't move in any direction.

Did You Know?

- Big or small, everything on Earth is pulled downward by gravity at the same rate. If you roll a marble and a tennis ball off a table at the same time, they will both hit the floor at the same time. Sound impossible? Try it!

- Our bodies are so used to gravity that our bones get weak without it. This happens to astronauts who spend a long time in space.

Mass and Gravity

Everything that has mass produces a gravitational field. That's the area around an object where its gravity has an effect. Even ordinary objects such as pencils and apples have gravitational fields. But the force in these fields is so small that we can't feel it or see it at work. It's too weak to cause anything around it to move.

The force of attraction between objects depends on their masses. The larger the mass of an object, the stronger the force of gravity between it and another object. Earth's pull on the moon is very strong compared with the pull of two pool balls on a pool table. That's because the moon's and Earth's masses are much larger than the mass of a pool ball.

But distance is also a factor. The farther two objects are away from each other, the weaker their gravitational attraction. This is true regardless of the masses of the two objects. Planets near each other have a stronger attraction than planets that are far apart.

Objects with small masses have small gravitational fields. Because of this, their gravitational attraction is also small.

Doin' an Ollie

Have you ever done an ollie on a skateboard? This basic jumping trick is named for its inventor, Alan "Ollie" Gelfand. If you've done an ollie, you were using Isaac Newton's laws of motion.

Skateboard tricks, even just riding a skateboard along a flat surface, require the use of force. To do an ollie, you need force from four sources. One is gravity, which gives weight to the rider and the board. The second force comes from one of the rider's feet, which pushes down on the tail of the board. That pushes the front of the board up. The third force is the ground's reaction when the tail hits the ground. That pushes the back end of the board up. A fourth force is caused when the rider's other foot moves forward and pushes down on the board. This makes the board level for landing.

The Force of Magnetism

Magnets exert a force on certain other materials, much like the force of gravity. Two objects don't have to touch each other for a magnetic force to exist. But the closer a magnet is to something it attracts, such as iron, the stronger the force.

Some materials that are drawn to magnets are iron, steel, nickel, and cobalt.

Magnets are surrounded by invisible lines of force. The lines are what is called a magnetic field. The field is where the magnet's force can be felt.

You can see where the lines are by using a magnet and some iron filings. Put a bar magnet—a magnet with a rectangular shape—under a piece of paper. Then sprinkle iron filings on top of the paper. The filings will move to line up along the lines of the magnetic field.

Every magnet has a north pole and a south pole. Opposite poles attract each other, while poles that are alike push each other away. If you break a magnet in half, it becomes two magnets, each with its own opposite poles.

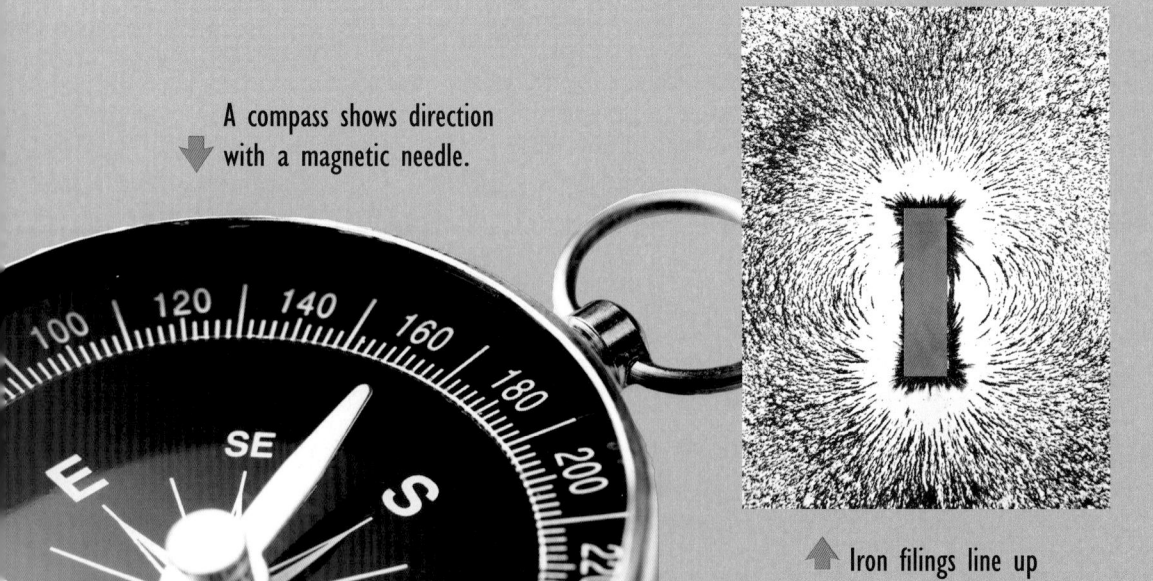

A compass shows direction with a magnetic needle.

Iron filings line up around a magnet.

Earth's Magnetic Field

If a bar magnet is hung by a string or placed on a piece of wood floating on water, it will swing around so that one end points north and the other south. That happens because Earth acts like a giant magnet, with a north pole and south pole. Earth's magnetic field moves the suspended magnet. This is how a compass works. Its needle is a magnet whose south pole always points toward Earth's north pole.

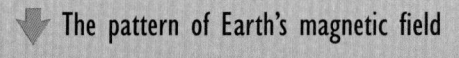
The pattern of Earth's magnetic field

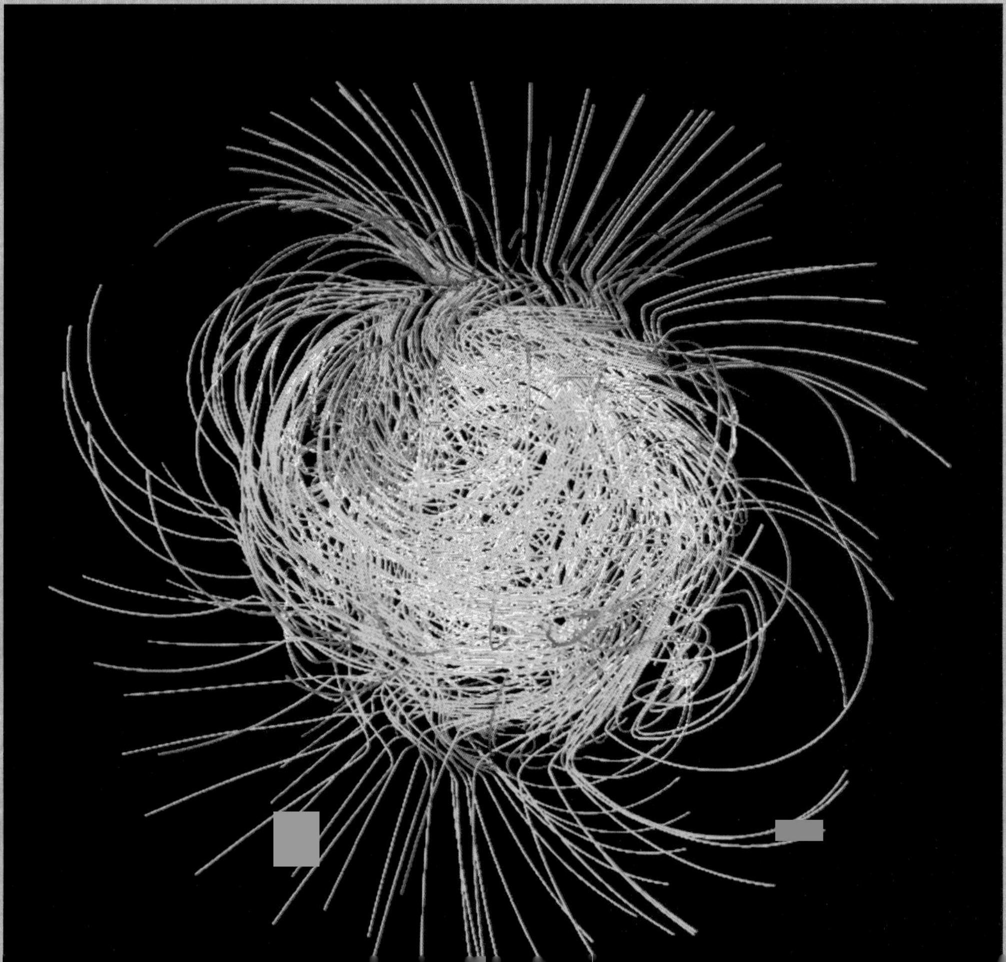

Electromagnetism

Electricity and magnetism are closely related, and they work together. The flow of electricity in a wire creates a magnetic field around the wire. The opposite is also true: Moving a wire loop inside a magnetic field creates a flow of electricity in the wire. What's happening is electromagnetism—the combination of electricity and magnetism.

You can make an electromagnet with a battery and some wire. Wrap the wire around an iron nail as many times as you can. Connect the ends of the wire to the ends of the battery, and the nail will be magnetized. Like any other magnet, it can pick up paper clips and other metal objects.

Did You Know?

A very strong electromagnet is used in magnetic resonance imaging scanners, which create images of the inside of a human body. Using MRI scans, doctors can check for problems without doing surgery.

What's That Static?

Stereos sometimes make a buzzing noise when cell phones are used near them. The static is caused by electromagnetic interference. The electromagnetic field created by the phone changes the electrical signal in the stereo's speakers.

They're Everywhere!

Electromagnets are used in many devices, including doorbells, security locks, metal detectors, and pumps for fish tanks.

⬆ Even a very small electromagnet can have many winds of copper wire.

Simple Machines

Natural forces such as gravity can prevent us from doing things on our own. When the ancient Egyptians built the pyramids, they needed to move huge blocks of stone to the top. Lifting them straight up would have required great strength. But a simple machine—a ramp or a series of ramps—made their work a lot easier. They had to move the blocks farther, but it took much less effort because they were moving them on a gradual incline. Their machine is called an inclined plane.

Machines make work easier by multiplying force. The lever, a simple machine, reduces the force required to do a job. It is a long bar that pivots on a stationary point called a fulcrum. If you push down on one end of the lever, the other end rises. The longer the lever, the more times a force can be multiplied. A seesaw is built for fun, not work, but it's an example of a lever.

Other simple machines are a pulley, a wheel and axle, a screw, and a wedge. These machines can be combined with one another to make more complex machines, such as a bicycle. You use many machines every day. Did you open a door today or climb stairs? If so, you used a simple machine.

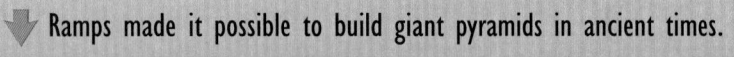
Ramps made it possible to build giant pyramids in ancient times.

Putting on the Brakes

Some machines stop a force instead of multiplying one. When your bicycle is speeding down the road, you might decide to stop it. When you apply the brakes, a machine slows the rotation of the wheels. Rough surfaces on the road and bumps on the tires catch on each other. That causes friction, a kind of rubbing, which brings your bike to a stop.

The brakes in cars are a lot different from bike brakes, but they are also machines, and they also use friction. A driver isn't strong enough to stop a car using muscles alone, so the car's brake system has machines that multiply the force on the brake pedal. Friction slows the turning of the car's wheels. The friction caused when the slowing tires rub on the road stops the car.

Science Activity

Measuring the Force of Gravity

A pendulum is a weight, hanging by a string, that can swing freely from side to side. As the pendulum swings, gravity slows it down. If you measure the time it takes for the swings, you can use a formula to figure out the force of gravity.

Materials

- string

- 2 ounces (57 grams) of modeling clay

- marker

- ruler

- laboratory stand and clamp (or strong sticky tape and a table or door frame)

- stopwatch

- sheet of paper

Procedure

Measurements in this experiment are in meters instead of feet because most scientists use the metric system.

1. Cut a piece of string so that it is 1.25 meters long.

2. Mold a lump of modeling clay onto one end of the string to make a pendulum.

3. Measure 1 meter up the string from the center of the clay blob. Mark the string with your marker. Tie the string to the lab stand (or tape it to a table or door frame) and clamp it at the 1-meter mark. The clay should swing freely.

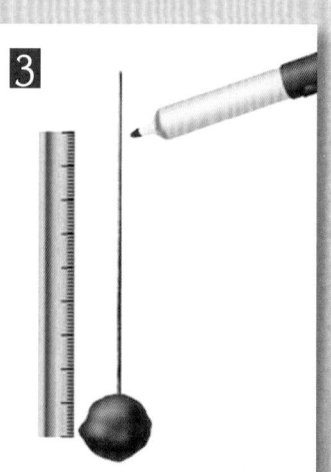

4. Hold the clay out to one side.

5. Let go of the clay and start the stopwatch.

6. Count 10 full swings of the pendulum (a swing is one time back and forth). Stop the stopwatch.

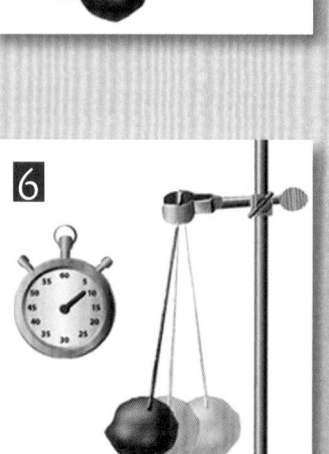

7 Record the time the pendulum took to make 10 swings.

8 Shorten the pendulum to 0.5 meter and repeat steps 4–7.

9 For each experiment, figure out the time (in seconds) that it took for one swing of the pendulum. You can do this by dividing the total time by 10. This is called the period of the pendulum.

10 Record your results.   [10]

pendulum length	time for 10 swings	time for 1 swing
1 meter		
0.5 meter		

11 Using the time it took for one swing in each experiment (calculated in step 9), find the force of gravity.

Use this formula:

$$\text{gravity} = \frac{(39 \times \text{length of string in meters})}{\text{swing time} \times \text{swing time}}$$

How do the two values for gravity compare? What effect does changing the length of the string have on the period of the pendulum?

acceleration—rate of increase of speed

atom—smallest particle of an element

drag—force that acts in a direction opposite to that of a moving object

electromagnetism—magnetism that is produced by an electrical current

electron—negatively charged particle that whirls around the nucleus of an atom

equilibrium—balance produced by opposing forces

force—factor, such as pushing or pulling, that causes an object to move or change speed or direction

friction—force that resists an object's motion

fulcrum—point on which a lever turns

gravity—force of attraction between objects, such as Earth's downward pull

inertia—tendency of an object to remain at rest or in motion unless acted upon by an outside force

lever—piece that pivots on a fulcrum and makes work easier by transferring and changing effort and motion

magnetic field—area where a magnet's force can be felt

mass—amount of matter contained in a substance

matter—particles of which everything is made

molecule—group of two or more atoms bonded together

neutron—particle in the nucleus of an atom that has no electric charge

newton—unit of measurement of force

pivot—to turn on a fixed point

proton—positively charged particle in the nucleus of an atom

speed—rate of motion

Important People in Physics

André Marie Ampère (1775–1836)
French physicist and mathematician who determined that electric currents produce magnetic fields; current strength is measured in amperes in his honor

Max Born (1882–1970)
German physicist who helped to develop quantum mechanics, a branch of physics that deals with the structure and behavior of atoms and smaller particles; won the Nobel Prize in physics in 1954

Marie Sklodowska Curie (1867–1934)
Polish-French physicist and chemist who was awarded two Nobel Prizes (in 1903 and 1911) for her pioneering work in radioactivity

John Dalton (1766–1844)
English chemist and physicist who developed the atomic theory of matter

Albert Einstein (1879–1955)
German-born American theoretical physicist and one of the greatest scientists in history; best known for his theories of relativity, especially one describing the relationship between mass and energy using the formula $E = mc^2$; won the Nobel Prize in physics in 1921

Michael Faraday (1791–1867)
English physicist and chemist who proposed the idea of magnetic lines of force, developed the first electrical generator, and pioneered the study of low temperatures

James Prescott Joule (1818–1889)
English physicist who helped to show that energy is not lost or gained when it changes form; basic unit of thermal energy is called the joule in his honor

Ernst Mach (1838–1916)
Austrian physicist who discovered that airflow is disturbed at the speed of sound; mach numbers, which show how fast something is moving compared with the speed of sound, are named for him

James Clerk Maxwell (1831–1879)
British physicist whose math equations were a basis for understanding electromagnetism; determined that light is electromagnetic radiation

Albert A. Michelson (1852–1931)
American physicist who showed that the speed of light is constant; his work laid the foundation for Albert Einstein's theories of relativity; in 1907 he became the first American to win a Nobel Prize in science when he received the prize in physics

Edward Morley (1838–1923)
American chemist and physicist who, with Albert Michelson, developed the interferometer to show that the velocity of light is a constant

J. Robert Oppenheimer (1904–1967)
American physicist who worked in astrophysics and directed the Manhattan Project, a U.S. government program that created the first atomic bomb

Max Planck (1858–1947)
German theoretical physicist who developed the quantum theory to explain the behavior of radiant energy; won the Nobel Prize in physics in 1918

Ernest Rutherford (1871–1937)
English physicist who studied the element uranium and became known as the father of nuclear physics

Forces and Motion Through Time

c. 1160	A perpetual motion machine is described; no successful perpetual motion machine has ever been created
1492	Christopher Columbus notices that the needle of a magnetic compass points in different directions at various longitudes
1581	Galileo Galilei studies swinging lamps, gaining knowledge that eventually leads to the pendulum and accurate clocks
1668	English mathematician John Wallis suggests the law of conservation of momentum, which leads to Isaac Newton's third law of motion
1676	English scientist Robert Hooke discovers that the stretch of a spring varies directly with its tension (Hooke's law)
1687	Newton establishes three laws of motion and the theory of gravity
1798	British scientist Henry Cavendish measures Earth's mass and determines gravity's constant
1800	Italian physicist Alessandro Volta invents a method for storing electricity in batteries
1837	Vermont blacksmith Thomas Davenport invents the electric motor
1885	German mechanical engineer Karl Benz designs and builds the first automobile powered by an internal-combustion engine
1905	Albert Einstein develops his general theory of relativity
1924	French scientist Louis de Broglie theorizes that particles of matter have the qualities of waves

1924	Romanian-born physicist Hermann Oberth explains how a rocket can produce enough force to overcome Earth's gravity
1935	Boulder (later renamed Hoover) Dam in Nevada is completed; in 1936 power is first transmitted to Los Angeles, California
1942	Italian physicist Enrico Fermi creates the first nuclear chain reaction
1945	The United States drops two atomic bombs on Japanese cities, ending World War II
1947	American physicists John Bardeen, Walter H. Brattain, and William Shockley at Bell Laboratories invent the transistor
1954	Scientists at Bell Laboratories invent the first useful solar cell
1957	The Soviet Union launches the first artificial Earth satellite, *Sputnik*
1969	American astronauts Neil Armstrong and Buzz Aldrin are the first humans to walk on the moon
1980	The first commercial geothermal plant in the United States begins operating in Southern California
1997	NASA's rover *Sojourner* begins gathering information about the geology of Mars
2008	Scientists in Europe send a beam of atomic particles around the world's biggest and most powerful particle accelerator, the Large Hadron Collider
2009	The U.S. spacecraft *Kepler* is launched to search for other planets where life can exist

Burnett, Betty. *The Laws of Motion: Understanding Uniform and Accelerated Motion*. New York: Rosen Publishing Group, 2005.

Nardo, Don. *Force and Motion: Laws of Movement*. Minneapolis: Compass Point Books, 2008.

Riley, Peter D. *Forces and Movement*. North Mankato, Minn.: Smart Apple Media, 2006.

Rosinsky, Natalie M. *Sir Isaac Newton: Brilliant Mathematician and Scientist*. Minneapolis: Compass Point Books, 2008.

Internet Sites

FactHound offers a safe, fun way to find Internet sites related to this book. All of the sites on FactHound have been researched by our staff.

Here's all you do:

Visit *www.facthound.com*

FactHound will fetch the best sites for you!

Index

Jane Weir

Jane Weir grew up in Leicester, England. She graduated from the University of Sheffield with a master's degree in physics and astronomy, but gained much of her practical knowledge of physics through rock climbing. Weir lives in Salisbury, England, where she works as a scientist for the British government.

Image Credits

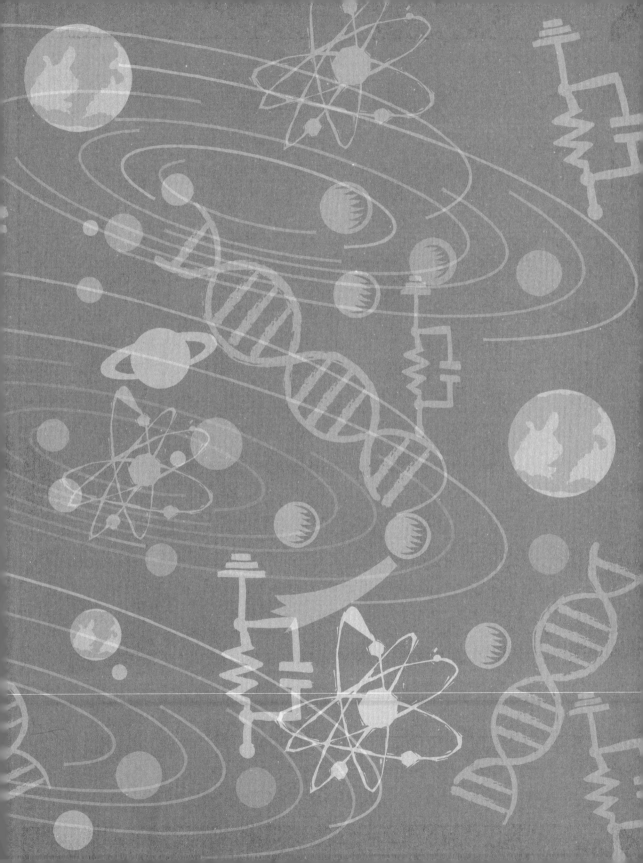